The Magic Rainbow Hug
Activity Book

JANET A. COURTNEY, PhD, LCSW

Illustrations By:

Kristen Krumenacker

And

Grace, age 8 and Benjamin, age 10

For the love and Play
and Imagination —
three 😊 of our greatest gifts,
with love,
Aunt Janet

This book is dedicated to children everywhere
who constantly remind us that
Play and Imagination
are two of life's greatest gifts

Acknowledgements

It is with the deepest of appreciation that I thank my husband, Robert D. Nolan, PhD, for hours and hours of listening, patience and feedback toward this project. Thanks to the gifted talents of Kristen Krumenacker for the border images, and the creative montage of weather elements found on the last pages of this book. Lots of Rainbow Hugs to Grace, age 8 and Benjamin, age 10 whose wonderful pictures created for the *Magic Rainbow Hug* were adapted for use in this activity book. My heartfelt appreciation goes to Rosanne Sammis, the remarkable Art teacher at the Benjamin School, for all of her time in guiding Grace and Ben with the drawings.

I am sincerely grateful to Nancy Luellan for pulling everything together with the final graphic design, pictorial text layout, and most especially for the amazing cover design. Thank you to Morgan Houck for his help with the technical support and compilation of this book.

Dear Kids. . .

This activity book is just for you, and goes along with the story, *The Magic Rainbow Hug*. In here, you can draw your favorite animal, what you like to do on a rainy day, what you might find at the end of the rainbow, and lots more. I also thought you might like to color some of the drawings from the story, so I picked out some of my favorites. I hope you like them too.

Before you begin, you can ask your Mom and Dad, or that special adult in your life, to copy this book for you. That way you can draw and color different pictures over and over again. (Most books you can't copy, but it is certainly okay for this one!)

After you draw your pictures~ if you want to~ maybe you can share them with your Mom, Dad, Grandmother, a teacher, a friend, your kitty cat or doggy. Know that there is always someone in your life that will be there to listen. You can even share your thoughts and pictures with me, Miss Janet! Lots of kids already do that, and I love to hear their stories. You can contact me at my website: www.myplaytherapy.com.

Rainbow Hugs to You,

Miss Janet

The little girl asks her Mother to tell her the story of
the Magic Rainbow Hug.

Draw what you imagine a Rainbow Hug looks like.

Jesse, Sophie and Oscar are happily playing
at Imagination Park on a sunny day.

Draw what you enjoy doing on a sunny day.

Oscar's favorite thing in the world is having his belly rubbed.

Sophie and Jesse love their puppy Oscar.
Draw a picture of an animal you love.

Jesse and Sophie look up to see the sun beginning to hide behind the clouds.

In the bubble beside each picture
write the word that says how you feel
in each kind of weather.

Sophie and Jesse run from the rain into the colorful stone castle.

Sophie and Jesse went to the castle to be safe.
Draw a place where you feel safe.

From inside the castle Sophie, Jesse and Oscar watch the storm.

In the bubble draw what you think Oscar is thinking.

The rain gets louder and louder and then it turns to icy hail.

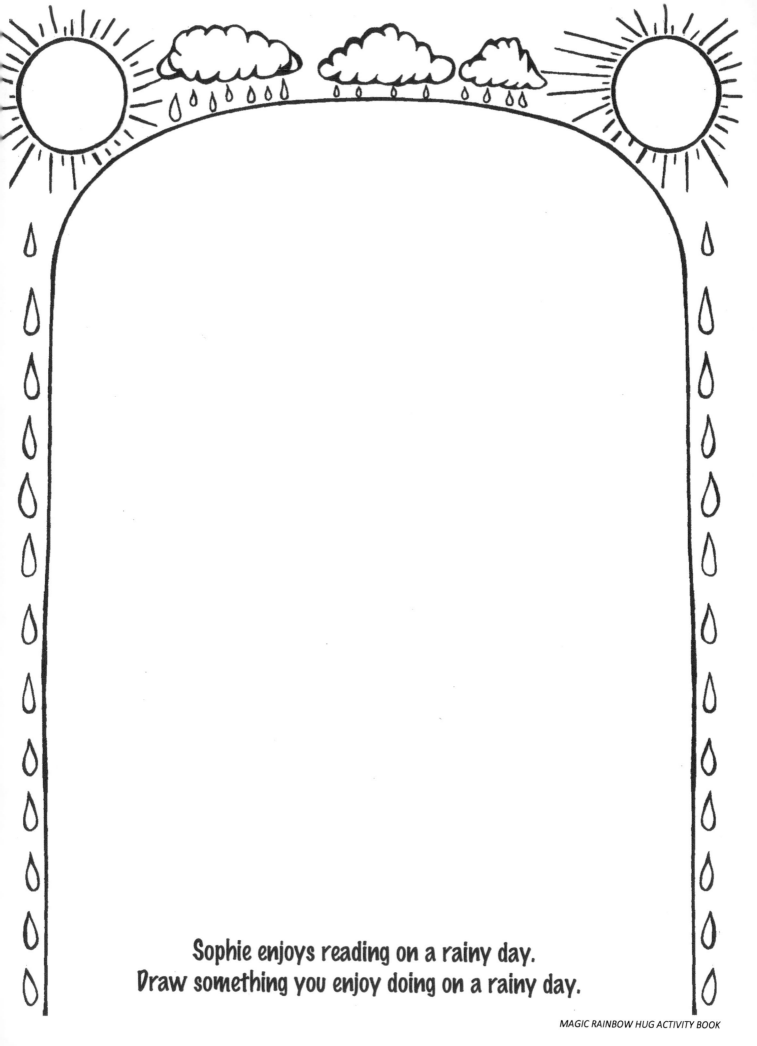

Sophie enjoys reading on a rainy day.
Draw something you enjoy doing on a rainy day.

Jesse and Sophie blow away all the dark clouds.

Do you have any worries?
Draw them all blowing away.

The storm is over. Sophie, Jesse and Oscar go back outside.

Draw a picture of something you would like to find at the end of the rainbow.

Sophie, Jesse and Oscar feel the magic of a Rainbow Hug.

Sophie and Jesse want to know
what rainbow colors went to your heart
after you felt a Rainbow Hug?
Color this heart with those colors.

The Mother and little girl share a Rainbow Hug.

Sophie loves getting a Rainbow Hug.
Draw a picture of someone you want to give
a Rainbow Hug.